C++ Game
Development Primer

Bruce Suthe

Apress®

C++ Game Development Primer

ISBN-13 (pbk): 978-1-4842-0815-1

ISBN-13 (electronic): 978-1-4842-0814-4

Trademarked names, logos, and images may appear in this book. Rather than use a trademark symbol with every occurrence of a trademarked name, logo, or image we use the names, logos, and images only in an editorial fashion and to the benefit of the trademark owner, with no intention of infringement of the trademark.

The use in this publication of trade names, trademarks, service marks, and similar terms, even if they are not identified as such, is not to be taken as an expression of opinion as to whether or not they are subject to proprietary rights.

While the advice and information in this book are believed to be true and accurate at the date of publication, neither the authors nor the editors nor the publisher can accept any legal responsibility for any errors or omissions that may be made. The publisher makes no warranty, express or implied, with respect to the material contained herein.

Managing Director: Welmoed Spahr
Lead Editor: Steve Anglin
Development Editor: Matthew Moodie
Technical Reviewer: Michael Thomas
Editorial Board: Steve Anglin, Ewan Buckingham, Gary Cornell, Louise Corrigan,
    James T. DeWolf, Jonathan Gennick, Jonathan Hassell, Robert Hutchinson,
    Michelle Lowman, James Markham, Matthew Moodie, Jeff Olson, Jeffrey Pepper,
    Douglas Pundick, Ben Renow-Clarke, Dominic Shakeshaft, Gwenan Spearing,
    Matt Wade, Steve Weiss
Coordinating Editor: Melissa Maldonado
Copy Editor: Teresa Horton
Compositor: SPi Global
Indexer: SPi Global
Artist: SPi Global
Cover Designer: Anna Ishchenko

Distributed to the book trade worldwide by Springer Science+Business Media New York, 233 Spring Street, 6th Floor, New York, NY 10013. Phone 1-800-SPRINGER, fax (201) 348-4505, e-mail orders-ny@springer-sbm.com, or visit www.springeronline.com. Apress Media, LLC is a California LLC and the sole member (owner) is Springer Science + Business Media Finance Inc (SSBM Finance Inc). SSBM Finance Inc is a Delaware corporation.

For information on translations, please e-mail rights@apress.com, or visit www.apress.com.

Apress and friends of ED books may be purchased in bulk for academic, corporate, or promotional use. eBook versions and licenses are also available for most titles. For more information, reference our Special Bulk Sales–eBook Licensing web page at www.apress.com/bulk-sales.

Any source code or other supplementary material referenced by the author in this text is available to readers at www.apress.com. For detailed information about how to locate your book's source code, go to www.apress.com/source-code/.

Contents at a Glance

Contents

About the Author

Bruce Sutherland is a video game developer working at Firemonkey Studios in Melbourne, Australia. He is currently working on iOS and Android titles written in C++ for both platforms. Bruce has worked on Real Racing 3, the Dead Space series, and The Elder Scrolls: Oblivion among others in his nine-year video game development career.

About the Technical Reviewer

Michael Thomas has worked in software development for more than 20 years as an individual contributor, team lead, program manager, and Vice President of Engineering. Michael has more than 10 years of experience working with mobile devices. His current focus is in the medical sector, using mobile devices to accelerate information transfer between patients and health care providers.

About the Technical Reviewer

Acknowledgments

I'd like to thank the team at Apress, especially Melissa Maldonado and Michael Thomas, for all of their help in putting together this book. I'd also like to thank my wife, Claire, for her patience and understanding while I spent much of my time writing video game code, at work and at home.

Introduction

This book is designed to give you a brief introduction to some likely topics that you will encounter as you pursue a career in video game development. Knowing a programming language is only part of the battle. Video game development is a diverse field that covers graphics programming, AI programming, UI programming and network programming. All of these fields are underpinned by a code understanding of how a computer operates to achieve the maximum performance possible for a given piece of hardware.

This book aims to give you an understanding of some of the first steps that a game developer will take after learning a programming language such as C++. These topics cover areas such as concurrent programming and the C++ memory model.

I hope you enjoy this introduction the video game development.

Chapter 1

Managing Memory for Game Developers

Memory management is a very important topic in game development. All games go through a period in development where memory is running low and the art team would like some more for extra textures or meshes. The way memory is laid out is also vitally important to the performance of your game. Understanding when to use stack memory, when to use heap memory, and the performance implications of each are important factors in to being able to optimize your programs for cache coherency and data locality. Before you can understand how to approach those problems you will need to understand the different places where C++ programs can store their data.

There are three places in C++ where you can store your memory: There is a static space for storing static variables, the stack for storing local variables and function parameters, and the heap (or free store) from where you can dynamically allocate memory for different purposes.

Static Memory

Static memory is handled by the compiler and there isn't much to say about it. When you build your program using the compiler, it sets aside a chunk of memory large enough to store all of the static and global variables defined in your program. This includes strings that are in your source code, which are included in an area of static memory known as a string table.

There's not much else to say regarding static memory, so we'll move on to discussing the stack.

The C++ Stack Memory Model

The stack is more difficult to understand. Every time you call a function, the compiler generates code behind the scenes to allocate memory for the parameters and local variables for the function being called. Listing 1-1 shows some simple code that we then use to explain how the stack operates.

Listing 1-1. A Simple C++ Program

```cpp
void function2(int variable1)
{
        int variable2{ variable1 };
}

void function1(int variable)
{
        function2(variable);
}

int _tmain(int argc, _TCHAR* argv[])
{
        int variable{ 0 };
        function1(variable);

        return 0;
}
```

The program in Listing 1-1 is very simple: It begins with _tmain, which calls function1 which calls function2. Figure 1-1 illustrates what the stack would look like for the main function.

```
┌─────────────────────────────────────────┐
│          _tmain: variable= 0             │
└─────────────────────────────────────────┘
```

Figure 1-1. The stack for tmain

The stack space for main is very simple. It has a single storage space for the local variable named variable. These stack spaces for individual functions are known as *stack frames*.When function1 is called, a new stack frame is created on top of the existing frame for _tmain. Figure 1-2 shows this in action.

function1.variable= _tmain.variable

_tmain.variable= 0

Figure 1-2. The added stack frame for function1

When the compiler creates the code to push the stack frame for function1 onto the stack it also ensures that the parameter variable is initialized with the value stored in variable from _tmain. This is how parameters are passed by value. Finally, Figure 1-3 shows the last stack frame for function2 added to the stack.

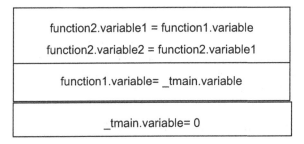

function2.variable1 = function1.variable

function2.variable2 = function2.variable1

function1.variable= _tmain.variable

_tmain.variable= 0

Figure 1-3. The complete stack frame

The last stack frame is a little more complicated but you should be able to see how the literal value 0 in _tmain has been passed all the way along the stack until it is eventually used to initialize variable2 in function2.

The remaining stack operations are relatively simple. When function2 returns the stack frame generated for that call is *popped* from the stack. This leaves us back at the state presented in Figure 1-2, and when function1 returns we are back at Figure 1-1. That's all you need to know to understand the basic functionality of a stack in C++.

Unfortunately things aren't actually this simple. The stack in C++ is a very complicated thing to fully understand and requires a bit of assembly programming knowledge. That topic is outside the scope of a book aimed at beginners, but it's well worth pursuing once you have a grasp of the basics. The article "Programmers Disassemble" in the September 2012 edition of *Game Developer Magazine* is an excellent introductory article on the operation of the x86 stack and well worth a read, available free from http://www.gdcvault.com/gdmag.

This chapter hasn't covered the ins and outs of how references and pointers are handled on the stack or how return values are implemented. Once you begin to think about this, you might begin to understand how complicated it can be. You might also be wondering why it's useful to understand how the stack works. The answer lies in trying to work out why your game has crashed once it is in a live environment. It's relatively easy to work out why a game crashes while you are developing, as you can simply reproduce the crash in a debugger. On games that have launched, you might receive a file known as a crash dump, which does not have any debugging information and simply has the current state of the stack to go on. At that point you need to look out for the symbol files from the build that let you work out the memory addresses of the functions that have been called, and you can then manually work out which functions have been called from the addresses in the stack and also try to figure out which function passed along an invalid memory address of value on the stack.

This is complicated and time-consuming work, but it does come up every so often in professional game development. Services such as Crashlytics for iOS and Android or BugSentry for Windows PC programs can upload crash dumps and provide a call stack for you on a web service to help alleviate a lot of the pain from trying to manually work out what is going wrong with your game.

The next big topic in memory management in C++ is the heap.

Working with Heap Memory

Manually managing dynamically allocated memory is sometimes challenging, slower than using stack memory, and also very often unnecessary. Managing dynamic memory will become more important for you once you advance to writing games that load data from external files, as it's often impossible to tell how much memory you'll need at compile time. The very first game I worked on prevented programmers from allocating dynamic memory altogether. We worked around this by allocating arrays of objects and reusing memory in these arrays when we ran out. This is one way to avoid the performance cost of allocating memory.

Allocating memory is an expensive operation because it has to be done in a manner that prevents memory corruption where possible. This is especially true on modern multiprocessor CPU architectures where multiple CPUs could be trying to allocate the same memory at the same time. This chapter is not intended to be an exhaustive resource on the topic of memory allocation techniques for game development, but instead introduces the concept of managing heap memory.

Listing 1-2 shows a simple program using the new and delete operators.

Listing 1-2. Allocating Memory for a class Dynamically

```cpp
class Simple
{
private:
        int variable{ 0 };

public:
        Simple()
        {
                std::cout << "Constructed" << std::endl;
        }

        ~Simple()
        {
                std::cout << "Destroyed" << std::endl;
        }
};

int _tmain(int argc, _TCHAR* argv[])
{
        Simple* pSimple = new Simple();
        delete pSimple;
        pSimple = nullptr;

        return 0;
}
```

This simple program shows new and delete in action. When you decide to allocate memory in C++ using the new operator, the amount of memory required is calculated automatically. The new operator in Listing 1-2 will reserve enough memory to store the Simple object along with its member variables. If you were to add more members to Simple or inherit it from another class, the program would still operate and enough memory would be reserved for the expanded class definition.

The new operator returns a pointer to the memory that you have requested to allocate. Once you have a pointer to memory that has been dynamically allocated, you are responsible for ensuring that the memory is also freed appropriately. You can see that this is done by passing the pointer to the delete operator. The delete operator is responsible for telling the operating system that the memory we reserved is no longer in use and can be used for other purposes. A last piece of housekeeping is then carried out when the pointer is set to store nullptr. By doing this we help prevent our code from assuming the pointer is still valid and that we can read and write from the memory as though it is still a Simple object. If your programs are crashing in seemingly random and inexplicable ways, accessing freed memory from pointers that have not been cleared is a common suspect.

The standard new and delete operators are used when allocating single objects; however, there are also specific new and delete operators that should be used when allocating and freeing arrays. These are shown in Listing 1-3.

Listing 1-3. Array new and delete

```
int* pIntArray = new int[16];
delete[] pIntArray;
```

This call to new will allocate 64 bytes of memory to store 16 int variables and return a pointer to the address of the first element. Any memory you allocate using the new[] operator should be deleted using the delete[] operator, because using the standard delete can result in not all of the memory you requested being freed.

> **Note**   Not freeing memory and not freeing memory properly is known as a memory leak. Leaking memory in this fashion is bad, as your program will eventually run out of free memory and crash because it eventually won't have any available to fulfill new allocations.

Hopefully you can see from this code why it's beneficial to use the available STL classes to avoid managing memory yourself. If you do find yourself in a position of having to manually allocate memory, the STL also provides the unique_ptr and shared_ptr templates to help delete the memory when appropriate. Listing 1-4 updates the code from Listing 1-2 and Listing 1-3 to use unique_ptr and shared_ptr objects.

Listing 1-4. Using unique_ptr and shared_ptr

```
#include <memory>

class Simple
{
private:
        int variable{ 0 };
```

```
public:
        Simple()
        {
                std::cout << "Constructed" << std::endl;
        }

        ~Simple()
        {
                std::cout << "Destroyed" << std::endl;
        }
};

int _tmain(int argc, _TCHAR* argv[])
{
        using UniqueSimplePtr = std::unique_ptr<Simple>;
        UniqueSimplePtr pSimple1{ new Simple() };
        std::cout << pSimple1.get() << std::endl;

        UniqueSimplePtr pSimple2;
        pSimple2.swap(pSimple1);
        std::cout << pSimple1.get() << std::endl;
        std::cout << pSimple2.get() << std::endl;

        using IntSharedPtr = std::shared_ptr<int>;
        IntSharedPtr pIntArray1{ new int[16] };
        IntSharedPtr pIntArray2{ pIntArray1 };

        std::cout << std::endl << pIntArray1.get() << std::endl;
        std::cout << pIntArray2.get() << std::endl;

        return 0;
}
```

As the name suggests, unique_ptr is used to ensure that you only have a single reference to allocated memory at a time. Listing 1-3 shows this in action. pSimple1 is assigned a new Simple pointer and pSimple2 is then created as empty. You can try initializing pSimple2 by passing it pSimple1 or using an assignment operator and your code will fail to compile. The only way to pass the pointer from one unique_ptr instance to another is using the swap method. The swap method moves the stored address and sets the pointer in the original unique_ptr instance to be nullptr. The first three lines of output in Figure 1-4 show the addresses stored in the unique_ptr instances.

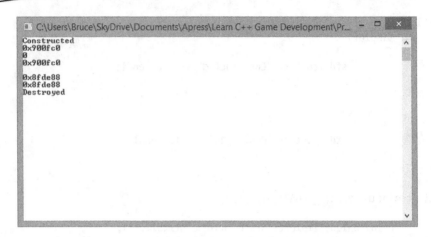

Figure 1-4. The output from Listing 1-4

This output shows that the constructor from the Simple class is called. The pointer stored in pSimple1 is then printed out before the call to swap is made. After the call to swap pSimple1 stores a nullptr that is output as 00000000 and pSimple2 stores the address originally held there. The very final line of the output shows that the destructor for the Simple object has also been called. This is another benefit we receive from using unique_ptr and shared_ptr: Once the objects go out of scope then the memory is freed automatically.

You can see from the two lines of output immediately before the line containing Destroyed that the two shared_ptr instances can store a reference to the same pointer. Only a single unique_ptr can reference a single memory location, but multiple shared_ptr instances can reference an address. The difference manifests itself in the timing of the delete call on the memory store. A unique_ptr will delete the memory it references as soon as it goes out of scope. It can do this because a unique_ptr can be sure that it is the only object referencing that memory. A shared_ptr, on the other hand, does not delete the memory when it goes out of scope; instead the memory is deleted when all of the shared_ptr objects pointing at that address are no longer being used.

This does require a bit of discipline, as if you were to access the pointer using the get method on these objects then you could still be in a situation where you are referencing the memory after it has been deleted. If you are using unique_ptr or shared_ptr make sure that you are only passing the pointer around using the supplied swap and other accessor methods supplied by the templates and not manually using the get method.

Writing a Basic Single Threaded Memory Allocator

This section is going to show you how to overload the new and delete operators to create a very basic memory management system. This system is going to have a lot of drawbacks: It will store a finite amount of memory in a static array, it will suffer from memory fragmentation issues, and it will also leak any freed memory. This section is simply an introduction to some of the processes that occur when allocating memory, and it highlights some of the issues that make writing a fully featured memory manager a difficult task.

Listing 1-5 begins by showing you a structure that will be used as a header for our memory allocations.

Listing 1-5. The MemoryAllocationHeader *struct*

```
struct MemoryAllocationHeader
{
        void* pStart{ nullptr };
        void* pNextFree{ nullptr };
        size_t size{ 0 };
};
```

This struct stores a pointer to the memory returned to the user in the pStart void* variable, a pointer to the next free block of memory in the pNextFree pointer, and the size of the allocated memory in the size variable.

Our memory manager isn't going to use dynamic memory to allocate memory to the user's program. Instead it is going to return an address from inside a static array. This array is created in an unnamed namespace shown in Listing 1-6.

Listing 1-6. The Unnamed namespace from Chapter1-MemoryAllocator.cpp

```
namespace
{
        const unsigned int ONE_MEGABYTE = 1024 * 1024 * 1024;
        char pMemoryHeap[ONE_MEGABYTE];
        const size_t SIZE_OF_MEMORY_HEADER = sizeof(MemoryAllocationHeader);
}
```

Here you can see that we allocate a static array of 1 MB in size. We know that this is 1 MB as the char type is one byte in size on most platforms and we are allocating an array that is 1,024 bytes times 1,024 KB in size for a total of 1,048,576 bytes. The unnamed namespace also has a constant storing the size of our MemoryAllocationHeader object, calculated using the sizeof function. This size is 12 bytes: 4 bytes for the pStart pointer, 4 bytes for the pNextFree pointer, and 4 bytes for the size variable.

The next important piece for code overloads the new operator. The new and delete functions that you have seen so far are just functions that can be hidden in the same way you can hide any other function with your own implementation. Listing 1-7 shows our new function.

Listing 1-7. The Overloaded new Function

```
void* operator new(size_t size)
{
        MemoryAllocationHeader* pHeader =
                reinterpret_cast<MemoryAllocationHeader*>(pMemoryHeap);
        while (pHeader != nullptr && pHeader->pNextFree != nullptr)
        {
                pHeader = reinterpret_cast<MemoryAllocationHeader*>
                (pHeader->pNextFree);
        }

        pHeader->pStart = reinterpret_cast<char*>(pHeader)+SIZE_OF_MEMORY_HEADER;
        pHeader->pNextFree = reinterpret_cast<char*>(pHeader->pStart) + size;
        pHeader->size = size;

        return pHeader->pStart;
}
```

The new operator is passed the size of the allocation we would like to reserve and returns a void* to the beginning of the block of memory to which the user can write. The function begins by looping over the existing memory allocations until it finds the first allocated block with a nullptr in the pNextFree variable.

Once it finds a free block of memory, the pStart pointer is initialized to be the address of the free block plus the size of the memory allocation header. This ensures that every allocation also includes space for the pStart and pNextFree pointer and the size of the allocation. The new function ends by returning the value stored in pHeader->pStart ensuring that the user doesn't know anything about the MemoryAllocationHeader struct. They simply receive a pointer to a block of memory of the size they requested.

Once we have allocated memory, we can also free that memory. The overloaded delete operator clears the allocations from our heap in Listing 1-8.

Listing 1-8. The Overloaded delete Function

```
void operator delete(void* pMemory)
{
        MemoryAllocationHeader* pLast = nullptr;
        MemoryAllocationHeader* pCurrent =
                reinterpret_cast<MemoryAllocationHeader*>(pMemoryHeap);
        while (pCurrent != nullptr && pCurrent->pStart != pMemory)
        {
                pLast = pCurrent;
                pCurrent = reinterpret_cast<MemoryAllocationHeader*>
                (pCurrent->pNextFree);
        }

        if (pLast != nullptr)
        {
                pLast->pNextFree = reinterpret_cast<char*>
                (pCurrent->pNextFree);
        }

        pCurrent->pStart = nullptr;
        pCurrent->pNextFree = nullptr;
        pCurrent->size = 0;
}
```

This operator traverses the heap using two pointers, pLast and pCurrent. The heap is traversed until the pointer passed in pMemory is matched against an allocated memory block stored in the pStart pointer in a MemoryAllocationHeader struct. Once we find the matching allocation we set the pNextFree pointer to the address stored in pCurrent->pNextFree. This is the point at which we create two problems. We have fragmented our memory by freeing memory potentially between two other blocks of allocated memory, meaning that only an allocation of the same size or smaller can be filled from this block. In this example, the fragmentation is redundant because we have not implemented any way of tracking our free blocks of memory. One option would be to use a list to store all of the free blocks rather than storing them in the memory allocation headers themselves. Writing a full-featured memory allocator is a complicated task that could fill an entire book.

> **Note** You can see that we have a valid case for using reinterpret_cast in our new and delete operators. There aren't many valid cases for this type of cast. In this case we want to represent the same memory address using a different type and therefore the reinterpret_cast is the correct option.

Listing 1-9 contains the last memory function for this section and it is used to print out the contents of all active `MemoryAllocationHeader` objects in our heap.

Listing 1-9. The `PrintAllocations` Function

```
void PrintAllocations()
{
        MemoryAllocationHeader* pHeader =
                reinterpret_cast<MemoryAllocationHeader*>(pMemoryHeap);

        while (pHeader != nullptr)
        {
                std::cout << pHeader << std::endl;
                std::cout << pHeader->pStart << std::endl;
                std::cout << pHeader->pNextFree << std::endl;
                std::cout << pHeader->size << std::endl;

                pHeader = reinterpret_cast<MemoryAllocationHeader*>
                (pHeader->pNextFree);

                std::cout << std::endl << std::endl;
        }
}
```

This function loops over all of the valid `MemoryAllocationHeader` pointers in our head and prints their `pStart`, `pNextFree`, and `size` variables. Listing 1-10 shows an example `main` function that uses these functions.

Listing 1-10. Using the Memory Heap

```
int _tmain(int argc, _TCHAR* argv[])
{
        memset(pMemoryHeap, 0, SIZE_OF_MEMORY_HEADER);

        PrintAllocations();

        Simple* pSimple1 = new Simple();

        PrintAllocations();

        Simple* pSimple2 = new Simple();

        PrintAllocations();

        Simple* pSimple3 = new Simple();
```

```
    PrintAllocations();

    delete pSimple2;
    pSimple2 = nullptr;

    PrintAllocations();

    pSimple2 = new Simple();

    PrintAllocations();

    delete pSimple2;
    pSimple2 = nullptr;

    PrintAllocations();

    delete pSimple3;
    pSimple3 = nullptr;

    PrintAllocations();

    delete pSimple1;
    pSimple1 = nullptr;

    PrintAllocations();

    return 0;
}
```

This is a very simple function. It begins by using the memset function to initialize the first 12 bytes of the memory heap. memset works by taking an address, then a value to use, then the number of bytes to set. Each byte is then set to the value of the byte passed as the second parameter. In our case we are setting the first 12 bytes of pMemoryHeap to 0.

We then have our first call to PrintAllocations and the output from my run is the following.

```
0x00870320
0x00000000
0x00000000
0
```

The first line is the address of the MemoryAllocationHeader struct, which for our first call is also the address stored in pMemoryHeap. The next line is the value stored in pStart, then pNextFree, then size. These are all 0 as we have not yet made any allocations. The memory addresses are being printed as 32-bit hexadecimal values.

Our first Simple object is then allocated. It turns out that because the Simple class only contains a single int variable, we only need to allocate 4 bytes to store it. The output from the second PrintAllocations call confirms this.

```
Constructed
0x00870320
0x0087032C
0x00870330
4

0x00870330
0x00000000
0x00000000
0
```

We can see the Constructed text, which was printed in the constructor for the Simple class and then that our first MemoryAllocationHeader struct has been filled in. The address of the first allocation remains the same, as it is the beginning of the heap. The pStart variable stores the address from 12 bytes after the beginning as we have left enough space to store the header. The pNextFree variable stores the address after adding the 4 bytes required to store the pSimple variable, and the size variable stores the 4 from the size passed to new. We then have the printout of the first free block, starting at 00870330, which is conveniently 16 bytes after the first.

The program then allocates another two Simple objects to produce the following output.

```
Constructed
0x00870320
0x0087032C
0x00870330
4

0x00870330
0x0087033C
0x00870340
4

0x00870340
0x0087034C
0x00870350
4

0x00870350
0x00000000
0x00000000
0
```

In this output you can see the three allocated 4-byte objects and each of the start and next addresses in each allocation header. The output is updated again after deleting the second object.

```
Destroyed
0x00870320
0x0087032C
0x00870340
4

0x00870340
0x0087034C
0x00870350
4

0x00870350
0x00000000
0x00000000
0
```

The first allocated object now points to the third and the second allocated object has been removed from the heap. A fourth object is allocated just to see what would happen.

```
Constructed
0x00870320
0x0087032C
0x00870340
4

0x00870340
0x0087034C
0x00870350
4

0x00870350
0x0087035C
0x00870360
4

0x00870360
0x00000000
0x00000000
0
```

At this point pSimple1 is stored at address 0x0087032C, pSimple2 is at 0x0087035C, and pSimple3 is at 0x0087034C. The program then ends by deleting each allocated object one by one.

Despite the problems that would prevent you from using this memory manager in production code, it does serve as a useful example of how a heap operates. Some method of tracking allocations is used so that the memory management system can tell which memory is in use and which memory is free to be allocated.

Summary

This chapter has given you a very simple introduction to the C++ memory management model. You've seen that your programs will use static memory, stack memory, and heap memory to store the objects and data to be used by your games.

Static memory and stack memory are handled automatically by the compiler, and you'll have already used these types of memory without having to do anything in particular. Heap memory has higher management overhead, as it requires that you also free the memory once you have finished using it. You've seen that the STL provides the unique_ptr and shared_ptr templates to help automatically manage dynamic memory allocations. Finally, you were introduced to a simple memory manager. This memory manager would be unsuitable for production code, but it does provide you with an overview of how memory is allocated from a heap and how you can overload the global new and delete methods to hook in your own memory manager.

Extending this memory manager to be fully featured would involve adding support for reallocating freed blocks, defragmenting contiguous free blocks in the heap, and eventually ensuring the allocation system is thread safe. Modern games also tend to create multiple heaps to serve different purposes. It's not uncommon for games to create memory allocators to handle mesh data, textures, audio, and online systems. There could also be thread-safe allocators and allocators that are not thread safe that can be used in situations where memory accesses will not be made by more than one thread. Complex memory management systems also have small block allocators to handle memory requests below a certain size to help alleviate memory fragmentation, which could be caused by frequent small allocations made by the STL for string storage, and so on. As you can see, the topic of memory management in modern games is a far more complex problem than can be covered in this chapter alone.

Chapter 2

Useful Design Patterns for Game Development

Design patters are like blueprints for your code. They are systems you can use to complete tasks that are very similar in nature that arise while you are developing games. Just as STL data structures are reusable collections that can be used when needed to solve specific problems, design patterns can be utilized to solve logical problems in your code.

There are benefits to using design patterns in your game projects. First, they allow you to use a common language that many other developers will understand. This helps reduce the length of time it takes new programmers to get up to speed when helping on your projects because they might already be familiar with the concepts you have used when building your game's infrastructure.

Design patterns can also be implemented using common code. This means that you can reuse this code for a given pattern. Code reuse reduces the number of lines of code in use in your game, which leads to a more stable and more easily maintainable code base, both of which mean you can write better games more quickly. This chapter introduces you to three patterns: the Factory, the Observer and the Visitor.

Using the Factory Pattern in Games

The factory pattern is a useful way to abstract out the creation of dynamic objects at runtime. A factory for our purposes is simply a function that takes a type of object as a parameter and returns a pointer to a new object instance. The returned object is created on the heap and therefore it is the caller's responsibility to ensure that the object is deleted appropriately.

Listing 2-1 shows a factory method that I have created to instantiate the different types of `Option` objects used in Text Adventure.

Listing 2-1. A Factory for Creating Option Instances

```
Option* CreateOption(PlayerOptions optionType)
{
        Option* pOption = nullptr;

        switch (optionType)
        {
        case PlayerOptions::GoNorth:
                pOption = new MoveOption(
                        Room::JoiningDirections::North,
                        PlayerOptions::GoNorth, "Go North");
                break;
        case PlayerOptions::GoEast:
                pOption = new MoveOption(
                        Room::JoiningDirections::East,
                        PlayerOptions::GoEast, "Go East");
                break;
        case PlayerOptions::GoSouth:
                pOption = new MoveOption(
                        Room::JoiningDirections::South,
                        PlayerOptions::GoSouth, "Go South");
                break;
        case PlayerOptions::GoWest:
                pOption = new MoveOption(
                        Room::JoiningDirections::West,
                        PlayerOptions::GoWest, "Go West");
                break;
        case PlayerOptions::OpenChest:
                pOption = new OpenChestOption("Open Chest");
                break;
        case PlayerOptions::AttackEnemy:
                pOption = new AttackEnemyOption();
                break;
        case PlayerOptions::Quit:
                pOption = new QuitOption("Quit");
                break;
        case PlayerOptions::None:
                break;
        default:
                break;
        }

        return pOption;
}
```

As you can see, the CreateOption factory function takes a PlayerOption enum as a parameter and then returns an appropriately constructed Option. This relies on polymorphism to return a base pointer for the object. The knock-on effect of this use of polymorphism is that any factory function can only create objects that derive from its return type. Many game engines manage this by having all creatable objects derive from a common base class. For our purposes, in the context of learning, it's better to cover a couple of examples. Listing 2-2 shows a factory for the Enemy derived classes.

Listing 2-2. The Enemy Factory

```
Enemy* CreateEnemy(EnemyType enemyType)
{
        Enemy* pEnemy = nullptr;
        switch (enemyType)
        {
        case EnemyType::Dragon:
                pEnemy = new Enemy(EnemyType::Dragon);
                break;
        case EnemyType::Orc:
                pEnemy = new Enemy(EnemyType::Orc);
                break;
        default:
                assert(false); // Unknown enemy type
                break;
        }
        return pEnemy;
}
```

If you were to create new inherited classes for these enemy types at some point in the future, you would only be required to update the factory function to add these new classes to your game. This is a handy feature of using factory methods to take advantage of polymorphic base classes.

So far all of the Option and Enemy objects in Text Adventure have been member variables within the Game class. This doesn't work too well with factory objects because the factory will create the objects on the heap, not using stack memory; therefore the Game class must be updated to store pointers to the Option and Enemy instances. You can see how this is done in Listing 2-3.

Listing 2-3. Updating Game to Store Pointers to Option and Enemy Instances

```
class Game
        : public EventHandler
{
private:
        static const unsigned int m_numberOfRooms = 4;
        using Rooms = std::array<Room::Pointer, m_numberOfRooms>;
        Rooms m_rooms;

        Player m_player;

        Option::Pointer m_attackDragonOption;
        Option::Pointer m_attackOrcOption;
        Option::Pointer m_moveNorthOption;
        Option::Pointer m_moveEastOption;
        Option::Pointer m_moveSouthOption;
        Option::Pointer m_moveWestOption;
        Option::Pointer m_openSwordChest;
        Option::Pointer m_quitOption;

        Sword m_sword;
        Chest m_swordChest;

        using Enemies = std::vector<Enemy::Pointer>;
        Enemies m_enemies;

        bool m_playerQuit{ false };

        void InitializeRooms();
        void WelcomePlayer();
        void GivePlayerOptions() const;  .
        void GetPlayerInput(std::stringstream& playerInput) const;
        void EvaluateInput(std::stringstream& playerInput);
public:
        Game();

        void RunGame();

        virtual void HandleEvent(const Event* pEvent);
};
```

Game now references the Option and Enemy instances via a type alias that is
defined in the respective Option and Enemy class definitions. These aliases
are shown in Listing 2-4.

Listing 2-4. The Option::Pointer and Enemy::Pointer Type Aliases

```cpp
class Option
{
public:
        using Pointer = std::shared_ptr<Option>;

protected:
        PlayerOptions m_chosenOption;
        std::string m_outputText;

public:
        Option(PlayerOptions chosenOption, const std::string& outputText)
                : m_chosenOption(chosenOption)
                , m_outputText(outputText)
        {

        }

        const std::string& GetOutputText() const
        {
                return m_outputText;
        }

        virtual void Evaluate(Player& player) = 0;
};

class Enemy
        : public Entity
{
public:
        using Pointer = std::shared_ptr<Enemy>;
private:
        EnemyType m_type;
        bool m_alive{ true };

public:
        Enemy(EnemyType type)
                : m_type{ type }
        {

        }

        EnemyType GetType() const
        {
                return m_type;
        }
```

```
bool IsAlive() const
{
        return m_alive;
}

void Kill()
{
        m_alive = false;
}
};
```

The Pointer aliases in both classes have been defined using the shared_ptr template. This means that once the instances have been created by the factories you will not need to worry about where the objects should be deleted. The shared_ptr will automatically delete the instance as soon as you no longer hold a shared_ptr reference.

Updating the Game class constructor is the next important change when using the two factory functions. This constructor is shown in Listing 2-5.

Listing 2-5. The Updated Game Constructor

```
Game::Game()
        : m_attackDragonOption{ CreateOption(PlayerOptions::AttackEnemy) }
        , m_attackOrcOption{ CreateOption(PlayerOptions::AttackEnemy) }
        , m_moveNorthOption{ CreateOption(PlayerOptions::GoNorth) }
        , m_moveEastOption{ CreateOption(PlayerOptions::GoEast) }
        , m_moveSouthOption{ CreateOption(PlayerOptions::GoSouth) }
        , m_moveWestOption{ CreateOption(PlayerOptions::GoWest) }
        , m_openSwordChest{ CreateOption(PlayerOptions::OpenChest) }
        , m_quitOption{ CreateOption(PlayerOptions::Quit) }
        , m_swordChest{ &m_sword }
{
        static_cast<OpenChestOption*>(m_openSwordChest.get())->
        SetChest(&m_swordChest);

        m_enemies.emplace_back(CreateEnemy(EnemyType::Dragon));
        static_cast<AttackEnemyOption*>(m_attackDragonOption.get())->
        SetEnemy(m_enemies[0]);

        m_enemies.emplace_back(CreateEnemy(EnemyType::Orc));
        static_cast<AttackEnemyOption*>(m_attackOrcOption.get())->
        SetEnemy(m_enemies[1]);
}
```

The constructor now calls the factory methods to create the proper instances needed to initialize the shared_ptr for each Option and Enemy. Each Option has its own pointer, but the Enemy instances are now placed into a vector using the emplace_back method. I've done this to show you how you can use the shared_ptr::get method along with static_cast to convert the polymorphic base class to the derived class needed to add the Enemy. The same type of cast is needed to add the address of m_swordChest to the m_openSwordChest option.

That's all there is to creating basic factory functions in C++. These functions come into their own when writing level loading code. Your data can store the type of object you'd like to create at any given time and just pass it into a factory that knows how to instantiate the correct object. This reduces the amount of code in your loading logic, which can help reduce bugs! This is definitely a worthwhile goal.

Decoupling with the Observer Pattern

The observer pattern is very useful in decoupling your code. Coupled code is code that shares too much information about itself with other classes. This could be specific methods in its interface or variables that are exposed between classes. Coupling has a couple of major drawbacks. The first is that it increases the number of places where your code must be updated when making changes to exposed methods or functions and the second is that your code becomes much less reusable. Coupled code is less reusable because you have to take over any coupled and dependent classes when deciding to reuse just a single class.

Observers help with decoupling by providing an interface for classes to derive which provide event methods that will be called on objects when certain changes happen on another class. The Event system introduced earlier had an informal version of the observer pattern. The Event class maintained a list of listeners that had their HandleEvent method called whenever an event they were listening for was triggered. The observer pattern formalizes this concept into a Notifier template class and interfaces that can be used to create observer classes. Listing 2-6 shows the code for the Notifier class.

Listing 2-6. The Notifier Template Class

```
template <typename Observer>
class Notifier
{
private:
        using Observers = std::vector<Observer*>;
        Observers m_observers;
```

```
public:
        void AddObserver(Observer* observer);
        void RemoveObserver(Observer* observer);

        template <void (Observer::*Method)()>
        void Notify();
};
```

The Notifier class defines a vector of pointers to Observer objects. There are complementary methods to add and remove observers to the Notifier and finally a template method named Notify, which will be used to notify Observer objects of an event. Listing 2-7 shows the AddObserver and RemoveObserver method definitions.

Listing 2-7. The AddObserver and RemoveObserver method definitions

```
template <typename Observer>
void Notifier<Observer>::AddObserver(Observer* observer)
{
        assert(find(m_observers.begin(), m_observers.end(), observer) ==
        m_observers.end());
        m_observers.emplace_back(observer);
}

template <typename Observer>
void Notifier<Observer>::RemoveObserver(Observer* observer)
{
        auto object = find(m_observers.begin(), m_observers.end(), observer);
        if (object != m_observers.end())
        {
                m_observers.erase(object);
        }
}
```

Adding an Observer is as simple as calling emplace_back on the m_observers vector. The assert is used to inform us if we are adding more than one copy of each Observer to the vector. The remove is achieved by using find to get an iterator to the object to be removed and calling erase if the iterator is valid.

The Notify method uses a C++ feature that you have not seen so far, *method pointers*. A method pointer allows us to pass the address of a method from a class definition that should be called on a specific object. Listing 2-8 contains the code for the Notify method.

Listing 2-8. The Notifier<Observer>::Notify *Method*

```
template <typename Observer>
template <void(Observer::*Method)()>
void Notifier<Observer>::Notify()
{
        for (auto& observer : m_observers)
        {
                (observer->*Method)();
        }
}
```

The Notify template method specifies a method pointer parameter. The method pointer must have a void return type and take no arguments. The type of a method pointer takes the following format.

```
void (Class::*VariableName)()
```

Class here represents the name of the class the method belongs to and VariableName is the name we use to reference the method pointer in our code. You can see this in action in the Notify method when we call the method using the Method identifier. The object we are calling the method on here is an Observer* and the address of the method is dereferenced using the pointer operator.

Once our Notifier class is complete, we can use it to create Notifier objects. Listing 2-9 inherits a Notifier into the QuitOption class.

Listing 2-9. Updating QuitOption

```
class QuitOption
        : public Option
        , public Notifier<QuitObserver>
{
public:
        QuitOption(const std::string& outputText)
                : Option(PlayerOptions::Quit, outputText)
        {

        }

        virtual void Evaluate(Player& player);
};
```

QuitOption now inherits from the Notifier class, which is passed a new class as its template parameter. Listing 2-10 shows the QuitObserver class.

Listing 2-10. The QuitObserver Class

```
class QuitObserver
{
public:
        virtual void OnQuit() = 0;
};
```

QuitObserver is simply an interface that provides a method, OnQuit, to deriving classes. Listing 2-11 shows how you should update the QuitOption::Evaluate method to take advantage of the Notifier functionality.

Listing 2-11. Updating QuitOption::Notifier

```
void QuitOption::Evaluate(Player& player)
{
        Notify<&QuitObserver::OnQuit>();
}
```

Now you can see the very clean template method call. This simple call will call the OnQuit method on every object that has been added as an observer on the QuitOption. That's our next step: The Game class is updated to inherit from QuitObserver in Listing 2-12.

Listing 2-12. The Game Class QuitObserver

```
class Game
        : public EventHandler
        , public QuitObserver
{
private:
        static const unsigned int m_numberOfRooms = 4;
        using Rooms = std::array<Room::Pointer, m_numberOfRooms>;
        Rooms m_rooms;

        Player m_player;

        Option::Pointer m_attackDragonOption;
        Option::Pointer m_attackOrcOption;
        Option::Pointer m_moveNorthOption;
        Option::Pointer m_moveEastOption;
        Option::Pointer m_moveSouthOption;
        Option::Pointer m_moveWestOption;
```

```
        Option::Pointer m_openSwordChest;
        Option::Pointer m_quitOption;

        Sword m_sword;
        Chest m_swordChest;

        using Enemies = std::vector<Enemy::Pointer>;
        Enemies m_enemies;

        bool m_playerQuit{ false };

        void InitializeRooms();
        void WelcomePlayer();
        void GivePlayerOptions() const;
        void GetPlayerInput(std::stringstream& playerInput) const;
        void EvaluateInput(std::stringstream& playerInput);
public:
        Game();
        ~Game();

        void RunGame();

        virtual void HandleEvent(const Event* pEvent);

        // From QuitObserver
        virtual void OnQuit();
};
```

The Game class inherits from QuitObserver, now has a destructor, and overloads the OnQuit method. Listing 2-13 shows how the constructor and destructor are responsible for adding and removing the class as a listener to QuitOption.

Listing 2-13. The Game Class Constructor and Destructor

```
Game::Game()
: m_attackDragonOption{ CreateOption(PlayerOptions::AttackEnemy) }
, m_attackOrcOption{ CreateOption(PlayerOptions::AttackEnemy) }
, m_moveNorthOption{ CreateOption(PlayerOptions::GoNorth) }
, m_moveEastOption{ CreateOption(PlayerOptions::GoEast) }
, m_moveSouthOption{ CreateOption(PlayerOptions::GoSouth) }
, m_moveWestOption{ CreateOption(PlayerOptions::GoWest) }
, m_openSwordChest{ CreateOption(PlayerOptions::OpenChest) }
, m_quitOption{ CreateOption(PlayerOptions::Quit) }
, m_swordChest{ &m_sword }
{
        static_cast<OpenChestOption*>(m_openSwordChest.get())->
        SetChest(&m_swordChest);
```

```
        m_enemies.emplace_back(CreateEnemy(EnemyType::Dragon));
        static_cast<AttackEnemyOption*>(m_attackDragonOption.get())->
        SetEnemy(m_enemies[0]);

        m_enemies.emplace_back(CreateEnemy(EnemyType::Orc));
        static_cast<AttackEnemyOption*>(m_attackOrcOption.get())->
        SetEnemy(m_enemies[1]);

        static_cast<QuitOption*>(m_quitOption.get())->AddObserver(this);
}

Game::~Game()
{
        static_cast<QuitOption*>(m_quitOption.get())->RemoveObserver(this);
}
```

The last line of the constructor registers the object as an observer on
m_quitOption and removes itself in the destructor. The last update in
Listing 2-14 implements the OnQuit method.

Listing 2-14. The Game::OnQuit Method

```
void Game::OnQuit()
{
        m_playerQuit = true;
}
```

This is all there is to implementing the observer pattern. This has achieved
another decoupling between the QuitOption class and any other classes
in the game that need to know about quit events. The observer class is
especially useful when creating game framework code for systems such as
online features. You can imagine a situation where you implement a class
to download leaderboards from a web server. This class could be used in
multiple game projects and each individual game could simply implement
its own class to observe the downloader and act appropriately when the
leaderboard data has been received.

Easily Adding New Functionality with the Visitor Pattern

One of the main goals of writing reusable game engine code is to try
to avoid including game-specific functionality in your classes. This can
be hard to achieve with a pure object-oriented approach, as the aim of
encapsulation is to hide the data in your classes behind interfaces. This
could mean that you are required to add methods to classes to work on data
that are very specific to a certain class.

We can get around this problem by loosening our encapsulation on classes that must interact with game code, but we do so in a very structured manner. You can achieve this by using the visitor pattern. A visitor is an object that knows how to carry out a specific task on a type of object. These are incredibly useful when you need to carry out similar tasks on many objects that might inherit from the same base class but have different parameters or types. Listing 2-15 shows an interface class you can use to implement Visitor objects.

Listing 2-15. The Visitor Class

```
class Visitor
{
private:
        friend class Visitable;
        virtual void OnVisit(Visitable& visitable) = 0;
};
```

The Visitor class provides a pure virtual method OnVisit, which is passed an object that inherits from a class named Visitable. Listing 2-16 lists the Visitable class.

Listing 2-16. The Visitable Class

```
class Visitable
{
public:
        virtual ~Visitable() {}

        void Visit(Visitor& visitor)
        {
                visitor.OnVisit(*this);
        }
};
```

The Visitable class provides a Visit method that is passed the Visitor object. The Visit method calls the OnVisit method on the Visitor. This allows us to make the OnVisit method private, which ensures that only Visitable objects can be visited and that we are always passing a valid reference to the OnVisit method.

The visitor pattern is very simple to set up. You can see a concrete example of how to use the pattern in Listing 2-17, where the Option class from Text Adventure has been inherited from Visitable.

Listing 2-17. The Updated Option Class

```
class Option
        : public Visitable
{
public:
        using Pointer = std::shared_ptr<Option>;

protected:
        PlayerOptions m_chosenOption;
        std::string m_outputText;

public:
        Option(PlayerOptions chosenOption, const std::string& outputText)
                : m_chosenOption(chosenOption)
                , m_outputText(outputText)
        {

        }

        const std::string& GetOutputText() const
        {
                return m_outputText;
        }

        virtual void Evaluate(Player& player) = 0;
};
```

The only change required is to inherit the Option class from Visitable. To take advantage of this, a Visitor named EvaluateVisitor is created in Listing 2-18.

Listing 2-18. The EvaluateVisitor Class

```
class EvaluateVisitor
        : public Visitor
{
private:
        Player& m_player;

public:
        EvaluateVisitor(Player& player)
        : m_player{ player }
        {
            .
        }
```

```
virtual void OnVisit(Visitable& visitable)
{
        Option* pOption = dynamic_cast<Option*>(&visitable);
        if (pOption != nullptr)
        {
                pOption->Evaluate(m_player);
        }
}
};
```

The EvaluateListener::OnVisit method uses a dynamic_cast to determine if the supplied visitable variable is an object derived from the Option class. If it is, the Option::Evaluate method is called. The only remaining update is to use the EvaluateVisitor class to interface with the chosen option in Game::EvaluateInput. This update is shown in Listing 2-19.

Listing 2-19. The Game::EvaluateInput Method

```
void Game::EvaluateInput(stringstream& playerInputStream)
{
        PlayerOptions chosenOption = PlayerOptions::None;
        unsigned int playerInputChoice{ 0 };
        playerInputStream >>playerInputChoice;

        try
        {
                Option::Pointer option =
                        m_player.GetCurrentRoom()->
                        EvaluateInput(playerInputChoice);
                EvaluateVisitor evaluator{ m_player };
                option->Visit(evaluator);
        }
        catch (const std::out_of_range&)
        {
                cout << "I do not recognize that option, try again!" << endl
                << endl;
        }
}
```

As you can see, the code has been updated to call the Visit method on the Option rather than calling the Evaluate method directly. That's all we needed to do to add the Visitor pattern to the Text Adventure game.

This example isn't the best use of the Visitor pattern, as it is relatively simple. Visitors can come into their own in places such as a render queue in 3-D games. You can implement different types of rendering operations in Visitor objects and use that to determine how individual games render their 3-D objects. Once you get the hang of abstracting out logic in this way, you might find many places where being able to provide different implementations independently of the data is very useful.

Summary

This chapter has given you a brief introduction to the concept of design patterns. Design patterns are exceptionally useful as they provide a ready-made toolbox of techniques that can be used to solve many diverse problems. You've seen the Factory, Observer, and Visitor patterns used in this chapter, but there are many, many more.

The de facto standard textbook on software engineering design patterns is *Design Patterns: Elements of Reusable Object Oriented Software* by Gamma, Helm, Johnson, and Vlissides (also known as the "Gang of Four"). If you find this concept interesting, you should read their book. It covers the examples shown here as well as other useful patterns. Bob Nystrom, a former software engineer at EA, has provided a free online collection of design patterns relevant to game development. You can find his web site here: http://gameprogrammingpatterns.com/

You'll find many patterns relevant and helpful when trying to solve game development problems. They also make your code easier to work with for other developers who are also versed in the common techniques that design patterns provide. Our next chapter is going to look at C++ IO streams and how we can use them to load and save game data.

Chapter 3

Using File IO to Save and Load Games

Saving and loading game progress is a standard feature of all but the most basic games today. This means that you will need to know how to handle the loading and saving of game objects. This chapter covers one possible strategy for writing out the data you will need to be able to reinstate a player's game.

First we look at the SerializationManager class, which uses the STL classes ifstream and ofstream to read and write from files. Then we cover how to update the Text Adventure game to be able to save which room the player is in, which items have been picked up, which enemies are dead, and which dynamic options have been removed.

What Is Serialization?

It would be good to cover what serialization is before we serialize the game's different classes. Serialization in computer programming covers the process of converting data into a format that can be written out by the program and read in at a later point in time. There are three major systems in modern games that take advantage of serialization.

The first is the save game system that will also be the basis for this chapter. Classes are serialized into a binary data file that can be read by the game at a later point in time. This type of serialization is essential for players to be able to retain their game data between different runs of the game and even on different computers. Transferring saved games between different machines is now a key feature of Xbox Live, PlayStation Network, Steam, and Origin.

The second main use of serialization is in multiplayer gaming. Multiplayer games need to be able to convert game object state into a small a number of bytes as possible for transmission over the Internet. The program on the receiving end then needs to be able to reinterpret the stream of incoming data to update the position, rotation, and state of opponent players' and projectiles. Multiplayer games are also required to serialize the win conditions of the round players are participating in so that winners and losers can be worked out.

The remaining systems are more useful during game development. Modern game toolsets and engines provide the ability to update game data at runtime. Player properties such as health or the amount of damage dealt by weapons can be updated by game designers while the game is running. This is made possible using serialization to convert data from the tool into a data stream that the game can then use to update its current state. This form of serialization can speed up the iteration process of game design. I've even worked with a tool that allows designers to update all of the current connected players in a multiplayer session midround.

These aren't the only forms of serialization you will encounter during game development, but they are likely to be the most common. This chapter focuses on serializing game data out and in using the C++ classes ofstream and ifstream. These classes provide the ability to serialize C++'s built-in types to and from files stored in your device's file system. This chapter shows you how to create classes that are aware of how to write out and read in their data using ifstream and ofstream. It will also show you a method for managing which objects need to be serialized and how to refer to relationships between objects using unique object IDs.

The Serialization Manager

The SerializationManager class is a Singleton that is responsible for keeping track of every object in the game that can have its state streamed out or is referenced by another savable object. Listing 3-1 covers the class definition for the SerializationManager.

Listing 3-1. The SerializationManager Class

```
class SerializationManager
        : public Singleton<SerializationManager>
{
private:
        using Serializables = std::unordered_map<unsigned int,
        Serializable*>;
        Serializables m_serializables;

        const char* const m_filename{"Save.txt"};
```

```
public:
        void RegisterSerializable(Serializable* pSerializable);

        void RemoveSerializable(Serializable* pSerializable);

        Serializable* GetSerializable(unsigned int serializableId) const;

        void ClearSave();

        void Save();

        bool Load();
};
```

The SerializationManager class stores pointers to Serializable objects in an unordered_map. Each of the Serializable objects will be given a unique ID that is used as the key in this collection. The file name we would like to use for the save file is stored in the m_filename variable.

There are three methods used to manage the objects that are handled by the SerializationManager class. The RegisterSerializable, RemoveSerializable, and GetSerializable methods are shown in Listing 3-2.

Listing 3-2. The RegisterSerializable, RemoveSerializable, and GetSerializable Methods

```
void SerializationManager::RegisterSerializable(Serializable* pSerializable)
{
        assert(m_serializables.find(pSerializable->GetId()) ==
        m_serializables.end());
        m_serializables.emplace{ pSerializable->GetId(), pSerializable };
}

void SerializationManager::RemoveSerializable(Serializable* pSerializable)
{
        auto iter = m_serializables.find(pSerializable->GetId());
        if (iter != m_serializables.end())
        {
                m_serializables.erase(iter);
        }
}

Serializable* SerializationManager::GetSerializable(unsigned int
serializableId) const
{
        Serializable* pSerializable{ nullptr };
        auto iter = m_serializables.find(serializableId);
```

```
        if (iter != m_serializables.end())
        {
                pSerializable = iter->second;
        }
        return pSerializable;
}
```

These methods are all fairly straightforward and manage adding, removing, and retrieving Serializable addresses from the m_serializables unordered_map.

The Save method is responsible for looping over all of the Serializable objects and asking them to write their data to an ofstream object. Listing 3-3 shows the Save method and how the ofstream object is initialized and moved.

Listing 3-3. The SerializableManager::Save

```
void SerializationManager::Save()
{
        std::ofstream file{ m_filename };
        file << true;
        file << std::endl;
        for (auto& serializable : m_serializables)
        {
                Serializable* pSerializable = serializable.second;
                file << pSerializable->GetId();
                file << std::endl;
                pSerializable->OnSave(file);

                file << std::endl;
                file << std::endl;
        }
}
```

An ofstream object is initialized by passing it the file name you wish to write to. You can then use the standard << operator to write data to the file. The o in ofstream stands for output, the f for file, and stream for its ability to stream data, meaning we are working with an *output file stream*.

The Save method begins by writing out a true. This bool is used to determine if the save game has a reinstatable save game inside. We write out false later when the player has completed the game. Save then loops over all of the stored Serializable objects, writes out their unique ID, and calls the OnSave method. The std::endl is being written out just to make the text file a little more readable and easier to debug.

The opposite action to Save is Load, shown in Listing 3-4.

Listing 3-4. The SerializationManager::Load Method

```cpp
bool SerializationManager::Load()
{
        std::ifstream file{ m_filename };
        bool found = file.is_open();
        if (found)
        {
                bool isValid;
                file >> isValid;
                if (isValid)
                {
                        std::cout <<
                                "Save game found, would you like to load?
                                (Type yes to load)"
                                << std::endl << std::endl;
                        std::string shouldLoad;
                        std::cin >> shouldLoad;
                        if (shouldLoad == "yes")
                        {
                                while (!file.eof())
                                {
                                        unsigned int serializableId{ 0 };
                                        file >> serializableId;
                                        auto iter = m_serializables.
                                        find(serializableId);
                                        if (iter != m_serializables.end())
                                        {
                                                iter->second->OnLoad(file);
                                        }
                                }
                        }
                }
                else
                {
                        found = false;
                }
        }
        return found;
}
```

The Load method is a little more involved than Save. You can see that it is using an ifstream, *input file stream*, rather than an ofstream. The ifstream is initialized using the file name to load. The is_open method in ifstream is used to determine if a file with the given name was found. If the player has never played the game, then no save file will exist; this check ensures that we do not try to load a game when no save game exists.

The next check is used to determine if the save file that does exist has a valid save state inside. This is done using the >> operator, just as is done when using cin. This is what happens next when cin is used to ask the player if he or she would like to load the save game. If the player types anything but *yes,* then game will start without loading.

There is then a while loop that is checking if the eof method is returning true. The eof method is determining whether the method has hit the *end of file.* The inner section of this loop reads the unique ID from the file, retrieves the Serializable from the map, and then calls the OnLoad method on that object.

The last SerializationManager method is ClearSave, which is used to write out a file with false as its only value. Listing 3-5 shows this method.

Listing 3-5. The SerializationManager::ClearSave Method

```
void SerializationManager::ClearSave()
{
        std::ofstream file{ m_filename };
        file << false;
}
```

The SerializationManager class is fairly simple. The Serializable class is also straightforward and is listed in Listing 3-6.

Listing 3-6. The Serializable Class

```
class Serializable
{
        unsigned int m_id{ 0 };

public:
        explicit Serializable(unsigned int id)
                : m_id{ id }
        {
                SerializationManager::GetSingleton().
RegisterSerializable(this);
        }

        Serializable::~Serializable()
        {
                SerializationManager* pSerializationManager =
                        SerializationManager::GetSingletonPtr();
                if (pSerializationManager)
                {
                        pSerializationManager->RemoveSerializable(this);
                }
        }
```

```
        virtual void OnSave(std::ofstream& file) = 0;
        virtual void OnLoad(std::ifstream& file) = 0;

        unsigned int GetId() const { return m_id; }
};
```

The Serializable class is intended to be inherited by the classes you would like to be able to save between game sessions and is therefore implemented as an interface. This is achieved by making the OnSave and OnLoad method purely virtual.

Each Serializable also stores an ID in the m_id variable. The constructor and destructor automatically adds and removes the object from the SerializationManager object that it accesses via the Singleton pattern.

Saving and Loading Text Adventure

The first step toward being able to save and load the game is to create the SerializationManager. Listing 3-7 shows the updated main function.

Listing 3-7. The Updated main Function

```
int _tmain(int argc, _TCHAR* argv[])
{
        new SerializationManager();

        Game game;
        game.RunGame();

        delete SerializationManager::GetSingletonPtr();

        return 0;
}
```

Creating and deleting the SerializationManager in main ensures that it exists for the entirety of the Game::RunGame method. The game is saved when the player chooses to quit, and Listing 3-8 shows how this is achieved.

Listing 3-8. Saving the Game

```
void Game::OnQuit()
{
        SerializationManager::GetSingleton().Save();
        m_playerQuit = true;
}
```

A call to SerializationManager::Save is added to the Game::OnQuit method. The Load and ClearSave methods are added to Game::RunGame in Listing 3-9.

Listing 3-9. The Game::RunGame Method

```
void Game::RunGame()
{
        InitializeRooms();

        const bool loaded = SerializationManager::GetSingleton().Load();
        WelcomePlayer(loaded);

        bool playerWon = false;
        while (m_playerQuit == false && playerWon == false)
        {
                GivePlayerOptions();

                stringstream playerInputStream;
                GetPlayerInput(playerInputStream);

                EvaluateInput(playerInputStream);

                for (auto& enemy : m_enemies)
                {
                        playerWon = enemy->IsAlive() == false;
                }
        }

        if (playerWon == true)
        {
                SerializationManager::GetSingleton().ClearSave();
                cout << "Congratulations, you rid the dungeon of monsters!"
                << endl;
                cout << "Type goodbye to end" << endl;
                std::string input;
                cin >> input;
        }
}
```

The WelcomePlayer method is now updated to ask the players if they would like to load their save game in Listing 3-10.

Listing 3-10. Updating Game::WelcomePlayer

```
void Game::WelcomePlayer(const bool loaded)
{
        if (!loaded)
        {
                cout << "Welcome to Text Adventure!" << endl << endl;
                cout << "What is your name?" << endl << endl;

                string name;
                cin >> name;
                m_player.SetName(name);

                cout << endl << "Hello " << m_player.GetName() << endl;
        }
        else
        {
                cout << endl << "Welcome Back " << m_player.GetName()
                << endl << endl;
        }
}
```

WelcomePlayer now greets players with a Welcome Back message once the game has loaded and reinstated the name they entered when they first played the game.

The next change to the Game class code is to pass a unique ID into the constructor of each object we would like to be a Serializable. The Game constructor is one place where this happens, as shown in Listing 3-11.

Listing 3-11. The Game Class Constructor

```
Game::Game()
: m_attackDragonOption{
        CreateOption(
                PlayerOptions::AttackEnemy,
                SDBMCalculator<18>::CalculateValue("AttackDragonOption")) }
, m_attackOrcOption{
        CreateOption(
                PlayerOptions::AttackEnemy,
                SDBMCalculator<15>::CalculateValue("AttackOrcOption")) }
, m_moveNorthOption{
        CreateOption(
                PlayerOptions::GoNorth,
                SDBMCalculator<15>::CalculateValue("MoveNorthOption")) }
, m_moveEastOption{
        CreateOption(
                PlayerOptions::GoEast,
                SDBMCalculator<14>::CalculateValue("MoveEastOption")) }
```

```
, m_moveSouthOption{
        CreateOption(
                PlayerOptions::GoSouth,
                SDBMCalculator<15>::CalculateValue("MoveSouthOption")) }
, m_moveWestOption{
        CreateOption(
                PlayerOptions::GoWest,
                SDBMCalculator<14>::CalculateValue("MoveWestOption")) }
, m_openSwordChest{
        CreateOption(
                PlayerOptions::OpenChest,
                SDBMCalculator<20>::CalculateValue("OpenSwordChestOption"))
}
, m_quitOption{
        CreateOption(
                PlayerOptions::Quit,
                SDBMCalculator<10>::CalculateValue("QuitOption")) }
, m_swordChest{ &m_sword, SDBMCalculator<5>::CalculateValue("Chest") }
{
        static_cast<OpenChestOption*>(m_openSwordChest.get())->
        SetChest(&m_swordChest);

        m_enemies.emplace_back(
                CreateEnemy(
                        EnemyType::Dragon,
                        SDBMCalculator<6>::CalculateValue("Dragon")));
        static_cast<AttackEnemyOption*>(m_attackDragonOption.get())->
        SetEnemy(m_enemies[0]);

        m_enemies.emplace_back(
                CreateEnemy(
                        EnemyType::Orc,
                        SDBMCalculator<3>::CalculateValue("Orc")));
        static_cast<AttackEnemyOption*>(m_attackOrcOption.get())->
        SetEnemy(m_enemies[1]);

        static_cast<QuitOption*>(m_quitOption.get())->AddObserver(this);
}
```

As you can see, each factory function now takes a hashed string that is used to construct the object and supply a unique ID for the SerializationManager's unordered_map. This unique key is also useful for game objects to be able to save out their references to other objects. You can see this in Listing 3-12, in which the source code for Player::OnSave is shown.

Listing 3-12. The Player::OnSave Method

```
void Player::OnSave(std::ofstream& file)
{
        file << m_name;
        file << std::endl;
        file << m_items.size();
        file << std::endl;
        for (auto& item : m_items)
        {
                file << item->GetId();
                file << std::endl;
        }
        file << m_pCurrentRoom->GetId();
        file << std::endl;
}
```

The Player::OnSave method writes out the name the user supplied when beginning his or her game. It then writes out the number of items in the m_items collection. Each item's ID is written out and finally the m_pCurrentRoom ID is written out. The block of text in the save file for a player looks like the following:

```
1923481025
Bruce
1
3714624381
625001751
```

The first line is the unique ID of the Player object, followed by the m_name, the number of Items, the ID of the one item, and finally the ID of the Room the player was in at the time he or she quit.

The Player::OnSave method is mirrored by the Player::OnLoad method in Listing 3-13.

Listing 3-13. The Player::OnLoad Method

```
void Player::OnLoad(std::ifstream& file)
{
        file >> m_name;
        unsigned int numItems;
        file >> numItems;
        for (unsigned int i = 0; i < numItems; ++i)
        {
                unsigned int itemId;
                file >> itemId;
                Item* pItem =
                dynamic_cast<Item*>(
```

```
                        SerializationManager::GetSingleton().
                        GetSerializable(itemId));
                m_items.emplace_back{ pItem };
        }

        unsigned int roomId;
        file >> roomId;
        Room* pRoom =
                dynamic_cast<Room*>(
                        SerializationManager::GetSingleton().
                        GetSerializable(roomId));
        m_pCurrentRoom = pRoom->GetPointer();
}
```

The OnLoad method reads the m_name variable out of the file, then the number of items. There is then a for loop that reads out the IDs of each item and retrieves a pointer to the Item from the SerializationManager. Each Serializable pointer is converted into an Item pointer using a dynamic_cast.

The Room pointer is a little more challenging. The Player class does not store a raw pointer to the Room object; instead, a shared_ptr was used. Listing 3-14 shows how the Room class has been updated to store a shared_ptr to itself, which can be used to retrieve a valid shared_ptr when retrieving the object from the SerializationManager.

Listing 3-14. The Room Class

```
class Room
        : public Entity
        , public Serializable
{
public:
        using Pointer = std::shared_ptr<Room>;

        enum class JoiningDirections
        {
                North = 0,
                East,
                South,
                West,
                Max
        };

private:
        using JoiningRooms = std::array<Pointer,
        static_cast<size_t>(JoiningDirections::Max)>;
        JoiningRooms m_pJoiningRooms;
```

```
        using StaticOptions = std::map<unsigned int, Option::Pointer>;
        StaticOptions m_staticOptions;
        unsigned int m_staticOptionStartKey{ 1 };

        using DynamicOptions = std::vector<Option::Pointer>;
        DynamicOptions m_dynamicOptions;

        Pointer m_pointer{ this };
public:
        explicit Room(unsigned int serializableId);

        void AddRoom(JoiningDirections direction, Pointer room);
        Pointer GetRoom(JoiningDirections direction) const;

        Option::Pointer EvaluateInput(unsigned int playerInput);
        void AddStaticOption(Option::Pointer option);
        void AddDynamicOption(Option::Pointer option);
        void PrintOptions() const;

        virtual void OnSave(std::ofstream& file);
        virtual void OnLoad(std::ifstream& file);

        Pointer GetPointer() const { return m_pointer; }
};
```

Now any time any part of our code wishes to store a shared_ptr to a Serializable object, it should be retrieving the pointer from a shared place. The easiest place for this to be is on the object itself, which is registered with the SerializationManager via its unique ID.

The Room class has to save and load the state of its dynamic options. Listing 3-15 shows the save and load methods.

Listing 3-15. Room::OnSave and Room::OnLoad

```
void Room::OnSave(std::ofstream& file)
{
        file << m_dynamicOptions.size();
        file << std::endl;
        for (auto& dynamicOption : m_dynamicOptions)
        {
                file << dynamicOption->GetId();
                file << std::endl;
        }
}
```

```
void Room::OnLoad(std::ifstream& file)
{
        m_dynamicOptions.clear();

        unsigned int numDynamicOptions;
        file >> numDynamicOptions;
        if (numDynamicOptions > 0)
        {
                for (unsigned int i = 0; i < numDynamicOptions; ++i)
                {
                        unsigned int optionId;
                        file >> optionId;
                        Option* pOption =
                                dynamic_cast<Option*>(
                SerializationManager::GetSingleton().
                GetSerializable(optionId));
                        if (pOption)
                        {
                                Option::Pointer sharedPointer =
                                pOption->GetPointer();
                                m_dynamicOptions.emplace_back{ sharedPointer };
                        }
                }
        }
}
```

The OnSave method loops over all of the dynamic options and saves their unique IDs after saving the number of dynamic options the state has. The OnLoad method begins by clearing the existing dynamic options and then reinstates each option from the SerializationManager. Once again this is done using a dynamic_cast and retrieving a shared_ptr from the Option class instances.

The Chest class and the Enemy classes are the only other classes with added OnSave and OnLoad methods. These are used to save the m_isOpen and m_alive variables from these classes and are shown in Listing 3-16.

Listing 3-16. The Chest::OnSave, Chest::OnLoad, Enemy::OnSave, and Enemy::OnLoad Methods

```
virtual void Chest::OnSave(std::ofstream& file)
{
        file << m_isOpen;
}

virtual void Chest::OnLoad(std::ifstream& file)
{
        file >> m_isOpen;
}
```

```
virtual void Enemy::OnSave(std::ofstream& file)
{
        file << m_alive;
}

virtual void Enemy::OnLoad(std::ifstream& file)
{
        file >> m_alive;
}
```

These simple methods round out the last of the class changes to support the saving and loading of the Text Adventure game. At this point I'd encourage you to get the sample code from the accompanying web site and take a look at the execution of the program in your debugger to get a feeling for how the ability to be able to reference objects via a centralized system using unique IDs can be very useful.

Summary

This chapter has given you an overview of a simple mechanism for implementing the ability to save and load your games. The ifstream and ofstream classes provide a simple mechanism for writing and reading file data for your programs. These classes follow the usual conventions for stream types in C++.

One of the most important lessons to take away from this chapter is the fact that pointers are not transferrable from one game session to the next. This is true for trying to implement a loading and saving system and is also true for implementing a multiplayer game. Pointer addresses cannot be sent from one computer to another to refer to any given object. Instead objects need to be created with a consistent and persistent unique ID and registered with a centralized system, which ensures there are no key clashes and can provide access to objects wherever it might be needed in your code.

Chapter 4

Speeding Up Games with Concurrent Programming

Processor manufacturers have hit a ceiling on the number of cycles their CPUs can execute per second. This can be seen with modern CPUs in desktop computers, tablets, and mobile phones where CPU speeds are rarely seen over the 2.5 Ghz mark.

CPU manufacturers have taken to adding more and more cores to their CPUs to provide more and more performance. The Xbox One, PlayStation 4, Samsung Galaxy phones, and desktop CPUs all have access to eight CPU cores to execute programs. This means that programmers of modern software need to embrace multithreaded, concurrent programming if they wish their programs to get the most out of modern computing devices and feel fluid and responsive for their users. Game programmers have to think about concurrency even across different processors. The Xbox One and PlayStation 4 actually have dual quad-core CPUs, audio CPUs, and GPUs all executing code at the same time.

This chapter will introduce multicore CPU programming so that you can have a basic understanding of how C++ allows you to execute code on multiple threads, how to ensure that those threads share resources responsibly, and how to make sure that all of the threads are destroyed before your program ends.

Running Text Adventure in Its Own Thread

I'm going to show you how to create a thread in this section that will execute the Game::RunGame method. This will mean that the main game loop is running in its own execution thread and our main function is left to carry out other tasks. Listing 4-1 shows how to create a game thread.

Listing 4-1. Creating a Thread

```
#include "GameLoop.h"
#include <thread>

void RunGameThread(Game& game)
{
        game.RunGame();
}

int _tmain(int argc, _TCHAR* argv[])
{
        new SerializationManager();

        Game game;
        std::thread gameThread{ RunGameThread, std::ref{ game } };
        assert(gameThread.joinable());
        gameThread.join();

        delete SerializationManager::GetSingletonPtr();

        return 0;
}
```

C++ provides the thread class that will automatically create a native operating system thread and execute a function that you pass into its constructor. In this example, we are creating a thread named gameThread that will run the RunGameThread function.

RunGameThread takes a reference to a Game object as a parameter. You can see that we are using std::ref to pass the game object to gameThread. You need to do this because the thread class constructor makes a copy of the object being passed in. Once it has this copy and starts the thread, the destructor is called on the copy. Calling ~Game will call ~Player, which will unregister our m_player object from the SerializationManager. If this happens, our game will crash, as the m_player object will not exist whenever the game tries to load the user's save game. The std::ref object avoids this by storing a reference to the game object internally and making copies of itself. When the destructors are being called, they are called on the ref object and not on the object passed. This prevents the crash you would otherwise experience.

Execution continues on your original thread once the new thread has been created and is running the function you supplied. At this point you can carry out some other tasks. Text Adventure doesn't have any other jobs to complete at the moment, and therefore execution would carry on, delete the SerializationManager, and return. This would cause another crash because your gameThread would go out of scope and try to destroy your running thread. What you really want to happen is for _tmain to stop executing until the task being carried out in gameThread has completed. Threads complete when their function returns and in our case we will be waiting for the player to either quit or win the game.

You make a running thread wait for another by calling join on the other thread's object. The joinable method is supplied to make sure that the thread you would like to wait on is one that is valid and running. You can test this by placing a breakpoint on the delete SerializationManager line. Your breakpoint will not be hit until you complete your game.

That's all there is to creating, running, and waiting for threads in C++. The next task is to work out how to make sure that threads can share data between each other without causing issues.

Sharing Data Between Threads Using Mutexes

Multithreaded programming introduces problems. What happens if two threads try to access the same variables at exactly the same time? Data can be inconsistent, data can be wrong, and changes can be lost. In the very worst examples your programs will crash. The updated main function in Listing 4-2 shows an example of a program that would crash when both threads access the same functions at the same time.

Listing 4-2. A Version of _tmain That Would Crash

```
int _tmain(int argc, _TCHAR* argv[])
{
        new SerializationManager();

        Game game;
        std::thread gameThread{ RunGameThread, std::ref{ game } };
        assert(gameThread.joinable());
        while (!game.HasFinished())
        {
                // Stick a breakpoint below to see that this code
                // is running at the same time as RunGame!
                int x = 0;
        }
```

```
      gameThread.join();

      delete SerializationManager::GetSingletonPtr();

      return 0;
}
```

This code would crash because the Game::HasFinished method is being called repeatedly. It is guaranteed that both the main thread and the game thread would try to access the variables inside HasFinished at the same time. Listing 4-3 contains the Game::HasFinished method.

Listing 4-3. Game::HasFinished

```
bool HasFinished() const
{
      return (m_playerQuit || m_playerWon);
}
```

The Game class tries to write to the m_playerWon variable once every loop. Eventually the main thread will try to read the m_playerWon variable at the same time as the game thread is writing to it and the program will close. You solve this problem by using mutual exclusion. C++ provides a mutex class that blocks execution on multiple threads around accesses to shared variables. By adding the code from Listing 4-4 you can create a mutex in the Game class.

Listing 4-4. Creating a mutex

```
std::mutex m_mutex;
std::unique_lock<std::mutex> m_finishedQueryLock{ m_mutex, std::defer_lock
};
```

We have two parts to our mutex, the mutex itself and a wrapper template named unique_lock, which provides convenient access to the behavior of the mutex. The unique_lock constructor takes a mutex object as its main parameter. This is the mutex that it acts on. The second parameter is optional; if it is not supplied, the unique_lock obtains a lock on the mutex immediately but by passing std::defer_lock we can prevent this from happening.

At this point you might be wondering exactly how a mutex works. A mutex can be locked and unlocked. We class the process of locking a mutex as obtaining a lock. The unique_lock template provides three methods to work with the mutex: lock, unlock, and try_lock.

The lock method is a *blocking* call. This means that your thread's execution will stall until the mutex has been successfully locked by the thread you called lock from. If the mutex is already locked by another thread, your thread will wait until the mutex becomes unlocked before proceeding.

The unlock method unlocks a locked mutex. Best practice is to hold your lock for as few lines of code as possible. Generally this means that you should do any calculations you need before obtaining a lock, obtain the lock, write the result to the shared variable, and then unlock immediately to allow other threads to lock the mutex.

The try_lock method is a nonblocking version of lock. This method returns true if the lock was obtained or false if the lock was not obtained. This allows you to do other work, usually in a loop within the thread until such time that the try_lock method returns true.

Now that you have seen the code to create a lock, I can show you how to use the unique_lock template to prevent your Text Adventure game from crashing. Listing 4-5 uses the lock to protect access to the m_playerQuit and m_playerWon variables in the HasFinished method.

Listing 4-5. Updating Game::HasFinished with the unique_lock

```
bool HasFinished() const
{
        m_finishedQueryLock.lock();
        bool hasFinished = m_playerQuit || m_playerWon;
        m_finishedQueryLock.unlock();
        return hasFinished;
}
```

The HasFinished method now calls the lock method on m_finishedQueryLock before it calculates the value to be stored in the hasFinished variable. The lock is released before the return statement in the method to allow any waiting threads to be able to lock the mutex.

This is only the first step in being able to protect our program from crashes. The HasFinished method is called on the main thread but the m_playerWon and m_playerQuit variables are written to from the game thread. I have added three new methods to protect these variables in the game thread in Listing 4-6.

Listing 4-6. The Game::SetPlayerQuit and Game::SetPlayerWon Methods

```
void SetPlayerQuit()
{
        m_finishedQueryLock.lock();
        m_playerQuit = true;
        m_finishedQueryLock.unlock();
}
```

```
void SetPlayerWon()
{
        m_finishedQueryLock.lock();
        m_playerWon = true;
        m_finishedQueryLock.unlock();
}

bool GetPlayerWon()
{
        m_finishedQueryLock.lock();
        bool playerWon = m_playerWon;
        m_finishedQueryLock.unlock();
        return playerWon;
}
```

This means that we are required to update the Game::OnQuit method as shown in Listing 4-7.

Listing 4-7. The Game::OnQuit Method

```
void Game::OnQuit()
{
        SerializationManager::GetSingleton().Save();
        SetPlayerQuit();
}
```

The Game::OnQuit method now calls the SetPlayerQuit method, which uses the m_finishedQueryLock to protect the variable access. The RunGame method needs to be updated to use the SetPlayerWon and GetPlayerWon methods and is shown in Listing 4-8.

Listing 4-8. Updating Game::RunGame

```
void Game::RunGame()
{
        InitializeRooms();

        const bool loaded = SerializationManager::GetSingleton().Load();
        WelcomePlayer(loaded);

        while (!HasFinished())
        {
                GivePlayerOptions();

                stringstream playerInputStream;
                GetPlayerInput(playerInputStream);

                EvaluateInput(playerInputStream);
```

```
        bool playerWon = true;
        for (auto& enemy : m_enemies)
        {
                playerWon &= enemy->IsAlive() == false;
        }

        if (playerWon)
        {
                SetPlayerWon();
        }
    }

    if (GetPlayerWon())
    {
            SerializationManager::GetSingleton().ClearSave();
            cout << "Congratulations, you rid the dungeon of monsters!"
            << endl;
            cout << "Type goodbye to end" << endl;
            std::string input;
            cin >> input;
    }
}
```

The bold lines show the updates to this method to support the mutex protection around our shared variables. There's an attempt to follow best practice by using a local variable to work out if the player has won the game before calling the SetPlayerWon method. You could wrap the entire loop in a mutex lock mechanism, but this would slow your program, as both threads would be spending longer in a state where they were simply waiting for locks to be unlocked and not executing code.

This extra work is one reason why splitting a program into two separate threads does not give a 100% increase in performance as there is some overhead to waiting for lock to synchronize access to shared memory between the threads. Reducing these synchronization points is key to extracting as much performance as possible from multithreaded code.

Threads and mutexes make up a low-level view of multithreaded programming. They represent abstract versions of operating system threads and locks. C++ also provides higher level threading abstractions that you should use more often than threads. These are provided in the promise and future classes.

Using Futures and Promises

The future and promise classes are used in a pair. The promise executes a task and places its result in a future. A future blocks execution on a thread until the promise result is available. Fortunately C++ provides a third template to create a promise and future for us so that we don't have to manually do this over and over.

Listing 4-9 updates the Game::RunGame to use a packaged_task to load the user's save game data.

Listing 4-9. Using a packaged_task

```
bool LoadSaveGame()
{
        return SerializationManager::GetSingleton().Load();
}

void Game::RunGame()
{
        InitializeRooms();

        std::packaged_task< bool() > loaderTask{ LoadSaveGame };
        std::thread loaderThread{ std::ref{ loaderTask } };
        auto loaderFuture = loaderTask.get_future();
          while (loaderFuture.wait_for(std::chrono::seconds{ 0 })
        != std::future_status::ready)
        {
                // Wait until the future is ready.
                // In a full game you could update a spinning progress icon!
                int x = 0;
        }
        bool userSaveLoaded = loaderFuture.get();
        WelcomePlayer(userSaveLoaded);

        while (!HasFinished())
        {
                GivePlayerOptions();

                stringstream playerInputStream;
                GetPlayerInput(playerInputStream);

                EvaluateInput(playerInputStream);

                bool playerWon = true;
                for (auto& enemy : m_enemies)
                {
                        playerWon &= enemy->IsAlive() == false;
                }
```

```
            if (playerWon)
            {
                    SetPlayerWon();
            }
    }

    if (GetPlayerWon())
    {
            SerializationManager::GetSingleton().ClearSave();
            cout << "Congratulations, you rid the dungeon of monsters!"
            << endl;
            cout << "Type goodbye to end" << endl;
            std::string input;
            cin >> input;
    }
}
```

The first step was to create a function, LoadSaveGame, to be executed in another thread. LoadSaveGame calls the SerializationManager::Load method. The LoadSaveGame function pointer is passed into the packaged_task constructor. The packaged_task template has been specialized with the type bool(). This is the type of the function; it returns a bool and does not take any parameters.

Then std::ref is used to pass the packaged_task into a thread. When a packaged_task is passed to a thread it can be executed, as a thread object knows how to handle packaged_task objects. This is true because a packaged_task object overloads an operator, which allows it to be called just like a function. This overloaded function call operator calls the actual function used to construct the packaged_task.

The main thread can now call the get_future method on the packaged_task. A future is used in threaded programs to allow you to set up tasks that will provide returned values at some point in the *future*. You could call get immediately on the future, but as get is a blocking call, your thread would stall until the future result is available. Listing 4-9 shows an alternate implementation where wait_for is used to check if the future result is available.

The future::wait_for method takes a value from the std::chrono set of duration classes. In this case, we are passing in std::chrono::seconds{ 0 }, which means the method will return instantly with a result. The possible return values in our case come from the std::future_status enum class and are ready or timeout. The timeout value will be returned until the player's game is loaded or he or she chooses to start a new game. At that point we can call the future::get method, which stores the value returned from SerializationManager::Load, via the LoadSaveGame function passed to loaderTask.

That wraps up your brief introduction to multithreaded C++ programming.

Summary

In this chapter you have been introduced to some of the classes C++ provides to allow you to add multiple execution threads to your programs. You first saw how threads can be created to execute functions. Calling functions in this manner allows the operating system to run your threads on more than one CPU thread and speed up the execution of your program.

When you use threads you need to make sure that your threads do not conflict when accessing variables and sharing data. You saw that the mutex can be used to manually provide mutually exclusive access to variables. After showing a mutex in action, I then introduced you to the packaged_task template, which automatically creates a promise and a future to better manage your concurrent tasks at a higher level than the base thread and mutex.

Using threads like this can allow you to provide better responsiveness to players. They aren't particularly effective in this task in a text-based game, but they can be used to provide more CPU execution time per frame in a 3D graphics-based game or for situations such as having a constantly updating loading or progress bar when long-running tasks are executing on other CPUs. Better responsiveness or faster frame rates improve usability and players' perception of your games.

The next chapter in this book will show you techniques that you can use to write code that will compile on multiple platforms. This will be useful if you find yourself in a situation where you want to write games that can run on iOS, Android and Windows Phones, or Windows and Linux, or even consoles such as the Xbox One and PlayStation 4. You might even write a game that can run on all of these in the same way an engine such as Unity can.

Chapter 5

Supporting Multiple Platforms in C++

There will come a time in your game development career when you have to write code which will only work on a single platform. That code will have to be compiled out of other platforms. You will more than likely also have to find alternative implementations for each of the platforms you will be working on. Classic examples of such code can usually be found in interactions between your game and online login and microtransaction solutions such as Game Center, Google+, Xbox Live, PlayStation Network and Steam.

There can be more complicated problems between different platforms. iOS devices run on Arm processors, Android supports Arm, x86 and MIPS and most other operating systems can be run on more than a single instruction set. The problem which can arise is that compilers for each of these CPU instruction sets can use different sizes for their built-in types. This is especially true when moving from 32bit CPUs to 64bit CPUs, in these situations pointers are no longer 32 bits in size, they are in fact 64 bits. This can cause all sorts of portability problems if you assume that types and pointers are of a fixed size. These issues can be very difficult to track down and will usually cause either graphical corruption or you will see your programs simply crash at random times.

Ensuring Types are the Same Size on Multiple Platforms

Ensuring that your program uses the same size of types in your programs on multiple platforms will be easier that you might initially think. The C++ STL provides a header called cstdint which contains types which are of a consistent size. These types are:

```
int8_t and uint8_t
int16_t and uint16_t
int32_t and uint32_t
int64_t and uint64_t
```

The int8_t and uint8_t provide integers which are 8 bits or one byte in length. The *u* version is unsigned while the non-u version is signed. The other types are similar but of their equivalent fixed length. There are 16 bit versions, 32 bit and 64 bit versions of integers.

> You should avoid using the 64 bit integers for the time being unless you explicitly need numbers which cannot be stored within 32 bits. Most processors still operator on 32 bit integers when doing arithmetic. Even 64 bit processors which have 64 bit memory addresses for pointers still to normal arithmetic using 32 bit ints. 64bit values also use twice as much memory as 32bit values which increases the RAM required to execute your program.

The next problem which might arise is that the char type may not be the same on all platforms. C++ does not supply a fixed size char type so we need to improvise a little. Every platform I have developed games on has used 8 bit char types, so we're only going to account for that. We will however define our own char type alias so that if you ever do port code to a platform with chars larger than 8 bits then you will only have to solve the problem in a single place. Listing 5-1 shows the code for a new header, FixedTypes.h.

Listing 5-1. FixedTypes.h

```
#pragma once
#include <cassert>
#include <cstdint>
#include <climits>

static_assert(CHAR_BIT == 8, "Compiling on a platform with large char type!");
using char8_t = char;
using uchar8_t = unsigned char;
```

The FixedTypes.h file includes `cstdint` which gives us access to the 8 – 64 bit fixed width integers. We then have a static_assert which ensures that the CHAR_BIT constant is equal to 8. The CHAR_BIT constant is supplied by the `climits` header and contains the number of bits which are used by the char type on your target platform. This `static_assert` will ensure that our code which includes the FixedTypes header will not compile on platforms which use a char with more than 8 bits. The header then defines two type aliases, char8_t and uchar8_t which you should use when you know you specifically need 8 bit chars. This isn't necessarily everywhere. Generally you will need 8 bit char types when loading data which was written out using tools on another computer which did use 8 bit character values because the length of the strings in the data will have one byte per character rather than more. If you're not sure if you do or don't need 8 bits specifically, you're better sticking to always using 8 bit chars.

The last problem solved in the cstdint header is for using pointers on platforms with different sized pointers to integers. Consider the code in Listing 5-2.

Listing 5-2. An example bad pointer cast

```
bool CompareAddresses(void* pAddress1, void* pAddress2)
{
        uint32_t address1 = reinterpret_cast<uint32_t>(pAddress1);
        uint32_t address2 = reinterpret_cast<uint32_t>(pAddress2);
        return address1 == address2;
}
```

There are a handful of cases where you might be required to compare the values of two addresses and you could case the pointers to 32 bit unsigned ints to achieve this comparison. This code however is not portable. The following two hexadecimal values represent different memory locations on 64 bit computers:

```
0xFFFFFFFF00000000
0x0000000000000000
```

If you cast these two values to uint32_t the two hex values stored in the unsigned integers will be:

0x00000000
0x00000000

The CompareAddresses function would return true for two different addresses because the upper 32bits of the 64bit addresses have been narrowed without warning by reinterpret_cast. This function would always work on systems with 32bit pointers or less and only break on 64 bit systems. Listing 5-3 contains the solution to this problem.

Listing 5-3. An example of a good pointer comparison

```
bool CompareAddresses(void* pAddress1, void* pAddress2)
{
        uintptr_t address1 = reinterpret_cast<uintptr_t>(pAddress1);
        uintptr_t address2 = reinterpret_cast<uintptr_t>(pAddress2);
        return address1 == address2;
}
```

The cstdint header provides intptr_t and uintptr_t which are signed and unsigned integers with enough bytes to completely store an address on your target platform. You should always use these types when casting pointers into integer values if you would like to write portable code!

Now that we've covered the different issues we can encounter with different sized integers and pointers on different platforms, we'll look at how we can provide different implementations of classes on different platforms.

Using the Preprocessor to Determine Target Platform

Straight off the bat in this section, I'll show you a header file which defines preprocessor macros to determine which platform you are currently targeting. Listing 5-4 contains the code for the Platforms.h header file.

Listing 5-4. Platforms.h

```
#pragma once

#if defined(_WIN32) || defined(_WIN64)

#define PLATFORM_WINDOWS 1
#define PLATFORM_ANDROID 0
#define PLATFORM_IOS 0

#elif defined(__ANDROID__)

#define PLATFORM_WINDOWS 0
#define PLATFORM_ANDROID 1
#define PLATFORM_IOS 0

#elif defined(TARGET_OS_IPHONE)

#define PLATFORM_WINDOWS 0
#define PLATFORM_ANDROID 0
#define PLATFORM_IOS 1

#endif
```

This header achieves the task of converting preprocessor symbols provided by the Windows, Android and iOS build tools into single definitions which we can now use in our own code. The _WIN32 and _WIN64 macros are added to your build on Windows machines while __ANDROID__ and TARGET_OS_IPHONE exist when building Android and iOS applications. These definitions can change over time, an obvious example is the _WIN64 macro which did not exist before the 64 bit versions of the Windows operating system and this is the reason for wanting to create our own platform macros. We can add or remove from Platforms.h as we see fit without affecting the rest of our program.

I've updated the Enemy classes to have platform specific implementations to show you how you can out these platform specific classes into action. Listing 5-5 shows that the Enemy class has been renamed to EnemyBase.

Listing 5-5. Renaming Enemy to EnemyBase

```cpp
#pragma once

#include "Entity.h"
#include "EnemyFactory.h"
#include "Serializable.h"
#include <memory>

class EnemyBase
        : public Entity
        , public Serializable
{
public:
        using Pointer = std::shared_ptr<EnemyBase>;

private:
        EnemyType m_type;
        bool m_alive{ true };

public:
        EnemyBase(EnemyType type, const uint32_t serializableId)
                : m_type{ type }
                , Serializable(serializableId)
        {

        }

        EnemyType GetType() const
        {
                return m_type;
        }

        bool IsAlive() const
        {
                return m_alive;
        }

        void Kill()
        {
                m_alive = false;
        }

        virtual void OnSave(std::ofstream& file)
        {
                file << m_alive;
        }

        virtual void OnLoad(std::ifstream& file)
        {
                file >> m_alive;
        }
};
```

The class isn't pure virtual as we don't actually have any platform specific code to add as this is an exercise for illustrative purposes. You can imagine that a proper base class for platform abstraction would have pure virtual methods which would have platform specific code added.

The next step is to create three classes for our different platforms. These are shown in Listing 5-6.

Listing 5-6. WindowsEnemy, AndroidEnemy and iOSEnemy

```cpp
class WindowsEnemy
        : public EnemyBase
{
public:
        WindowsEnemy(EnemyType type, const uint32_t serializableId)
                : EnemyBase(type, serializableId)
        {
                std::cout << "Created Windows Enemy!" << std::endl;
        }
};

class AndroidEnemy
        : public EnemyBase
{
public:
        AndroidEnemy(EnemyType type, const uint32_t serializableId)
                : EnemyBase( type , serializableId )
        {
                std::cout << "Created Android Enemy!" << std::endl;
        }
};

class iOSEnemy
        : public EnemyBase
{
public:
        iOSEnemy(EnemyType type, const uint32_t serializableId)
                : EnemyBase(type, serializableId)
        {
                std::cout << "Created iOS Enemy!" << std::endl;
        }
};
```

These three classes rely on polymorphism to allow the rest of the program to work with the EnemyBase class rather than the platform specific implementations. The last problem to solve is how to create these classes, fortunately the Factory pattern gives us a ready-made solution. Listing 5-7 updates EnemyFactory to create the correct type of EnemyBase for our implementation.

Listing 5-7. Updating EnemyFactory with platform specific types

```
namespace
{
#if PLATFORM_WINDOWS
#include "WindowsEnemy.h"
        using Enemy = WindowsEnemy;
#elif PLATFORM_ANDROID
#include "AndroidEnemy.h"
        using Enemy = AndroidEnemy;
#elif PLATFORM_IOS
#include "iOSEnemy.h"
        using Enemy = iOSEnemy;
#endif
}

EnemyBase* CreateEnemy(EnemyType enemyType, const uint32_t serializableId)
{
        Enemy* pEnemy = nullptr;
        switch (enemyType)
        {
        case EnemyType::Dragon:
                pEnemy = new Enemy(EnemyType::Dragon, serializableId);
                break;
        case EnemyType::Orc:
                pEnemy = new Enemy(EnemyType::Orc, serializableId);
                break;
        default:
                assert(false); // Unknown enemy type
                break;
        }
        return pEnemy;
}
```

The CreateEnemy function itself has only changes in one way. Its return type is now EnemyBase rather than Enemy. This is the case because I've used a type alias to have the Enemy keyword map to the correct platform specific Enemy version. You can see this in action in the unnamed namespace before the function. I check each platform definition, include the appropriate header and finally add using Enemy = to set the type alias to the correct type.

The Factory pattern is the perfect method to use when you need to implement platform specific versions of classes. The Factory allows you to hide the implementation details of the creation of objects from the rest of your program. This leads to easier to maintain code and reduces the number of places in your codebase where you have to change things around to add new platforms. Reducing the time to port to a new platform could be a lucrative business opportunity and open up new potential revenue streams for your company.

Summary

This chapter has shown a handful of techniques that will be useful for your cross-platform game development projects. I'd recommend abstracting out everything that you know uses a platform specific API or any classes that require the inclusion of platform specific header files. Even if you start your game development project without a plan to port to another platform, it's always easier to decide to support more platforms if you have taken some basic precautions in the original version of the game. Adding platforms will become much easier once you get into the habit of always abstracting out platform specific code.

Classic areas where platform specific code can be found are graphics APIs such as DirectX, OpenGL, Mantle and Metal, file handling systems, controller support, online features such as achievements and friends lists, and store microtransaction support. All of these systems can be hidden behind your own class interface and a factory can be used to instantiate the correct version of the class at runtime. Compiler preprocessor flags should be used to prevent compile and link errors caused by the inclusion of code that will only work with a specific platform's APIs. An easy to understand example is that PlayStation 4 controller code will not compile in an Xbox One target.

Chapter 6

Text Adventure

The C++ programming language is a tool which will serve you well while trying to build video games. It provides low-level access to processors which allows you to write efficient code for a wide variety of computer processors.

This chapter gives a very brief overview of an old-school text adventure written in C++. The code provided is available online at the book's web page at `www.apress.com/9781484208151`. The code is intended to be an example of various C++ techniques rather than example of how commercial C++ code should be written.

An Overview of Text Adventure

A very simple text adventure game that you can now expand into a full game if you wish is supplied to accompany this book. Listing 6-1 shows the Game class definition. This class encapsulates all of the types of programming C++ provides.

Listing 6-1. The Game class Definition

```
class Game
        : public EventHandler
        , public QuitObserver
{
private:
        static const uint32_t m_numberOfRooms = 4;
        using Rooms = std::array<Room::Pointer, m_numberOfRooms>;
        Rooms m_rooms;
```

```
Player m_player;

Option::Pointer m_attackDragonOption;
Option::Pointer m_attackOrcOption;
Option::Pointer m_moveNorthOption;
Option::Pointer m_moveEastOption;
Option::Pointer m_moveSouthOption;
Option::Pointer m_moveWestOption;
Option::Pointer m_openSwordChest;
Option::Pointer m_quitOption;

Sword m_sword;
Chest m_swordChest;

using Enemies = std::vector<EnemyBase::Pointer>;
Enemies m_enemies;

std::mutex m_mutex;
mutable std::unique_lock<std::mutex> m_finishedQueryLock{ m_mutex,
std::defer_lock };
bool m_playerQuit{ false };
void SetPlayerQuit()
{
        m_finishedQueryLock.lock();
        m_playerQuit = true;
        m_finishedQueryLock.unlock();
}

bool m_playerWon{ false };
void SetPlayerWon()
{
        m_finishedQueryLock.lock();
        m_playerWon = true;
        m_finishedQueryLock.unlock();
}

bool GetPlayerWon()
{
        m_finishedQueryLock.lock();
        bool playerWon = m_playerWon;
        m_finishedQueryLock.unlock();
        return playerWon;
}

void InitializeRooms();
void WelcomePlayer(const bool loaded);
void GivePlayerOptions() const;
void GetPlayerInput(std::stringstream& playerInput) const;
void EvaluateInput(std::stringstream& playerInput);
```

```
public:
        Game();
        virtual ~Game();

        void RunGame();

        virtual void HandleEvent(const Event* pEvent);

        // From QuitObserver
        virtual void OnQuit();

        bool HasFinished() const
        {
                m_finishedQueryLock.lock();
                bool hasFinished = m_playerQuit || m_playerWon;
                m_finishedQueryLock.unlock();
                return hasFinished;
        }
};
```

The Game class shows how you can construct classes in C++. There is a parent class from which Game derives. This class provides an interface which includes virtual methods. The Game class overrides these virtual methods with specific instances of its own. A perfect example of this is the HandleEvent method.

Game also shows how you can specialize STL templates for your own uses. There is an array of Room::Pointer instances as well as a vector of EnemyBase::Pointer instances. These types of pointers are created using type aliases. Type aliases in C++ allow you to create your own named types and are generally a good idea. If you ever need to change the type of an object at a later date you can get away with just changing the type alias. If you hadn't used an alias you would be required to manually change every location where the type had been used.

There is also a mutex present in the Game class. This mutex is a clue to the fact that C++ allows you to write programs which can execute on multiple CPU cores at once. A mutex is a mutual exclusion object which allows you to ensure that only a single thread is accessing a single variable at a time.

Listing 6-2 contains the final source for the Game::RunGame method. This method consists of code that shows how you can iterate over collections and use futures.

Listing 6-2. The Game::RunGame method

```cpp
void Game::RunGame()
{
        InitializeRooms();

        std::packaged_task< bool() > loaderTask{ LoadSaveGame };
        std::thread loaderThread{ std::ref{ loaderTask } };
        auto loaderFuture = loaderTask.get_future();
        while (loaderFuture.wait_for(std::chrono::seconds{ 0 }) !=
        std::future_status::ready)
        {
                // Wait until the future is ready.
                // In a full game you could update a spinning progress icon!
                int32_t x = 0;
        }
        bool userSaveLoaded = loaderFuture.get();
        loaderThread.join();
        WelcomePlayer(userSaveLoaded);

        while (!HasFinished())
        {
                GivePlayerOptions();

                stringstream playerInputStream;
                GetPlayerInput(playerInputStream);

                EvaluateInput(playerInputStream);

                bool playerWon = true;
                for (auto& enemy : m_enemies)
                {
                        playerWon &= enemy->IsAlive() == false;
                }

                if (playerWon)
                {
                        SetPlayerWon();
                }
        }

        if (GetPlayerWon())
        {
                SerializationManager::GetSingleton().ClearSave();
                cout << "Congratulations, you rid the dungeon of monsters!"
                << endl;
```

```
            cout << "Type goodbye to end" << endl;
            std::string input;
            cin >> input;
        }
    }
}
```

The range based for loop can be used in conjunction with the auto keyword to provide easy, portable iteration over many STL collections. You can see it in action in RunGame where there is a loop over the m_enemies vector.

A paired_task is used to execute save game loading on a separate thread of execution. The std::thread::get_future method is used to acquire a future object that lets you know when the task you were executing has been completed. This approach to loading can be used to allow you to load games whilst updating a dynamic loading screen.

There is also an example of how to use cin and cout to read player input and write out messages to the console. Input and output are fundamental concepts for game developers as they are essential to providing the interactivity which players expect from games.

Summary

Game development is a fun but demanding field to enter. There are many areas to explore, learn and attempt to master. Very few people become proficient in all areas of game development however their programming skills are usually transferable. Programmers can specialize in graphics programming, network programming, gameplay programming or other fields such as audio and animation. There will never be a shortage of tasks for programmers to undertake as most large games are written in C++ with code bases which have been around for ten to twenty years. Engines such as Cryengine, Unreal and Unity are written in C++ and provide support for scripting languages to create game logic. C++ is a perfect choice for someone looking to begin a career in game development which will take them into a AAA game development studio at some point.

I hope you've found this book an enjoyable entry into your journey down the path of your chosen career.

Index

Get the eBook for only $10!

> Now you can take the weightless companion with you anywhere, anytime. Your purchase of this book entitles you to 3 electronic versions for only $10.

This Apress title will prove so indispensible that you'll want to carry it with you everywhere, which is why we are offering the eBook in 3 formats for only $10 if you have already purchased the print book.

Convenient and fully searchable, the PDF version enables you to easily find and copy code—or perform examples by quickly toggling between instructions and   applications. The MOBI format is ideal for your Kindle, while the ePUB can be utilized on a variety of mobile devices.

Go to www.apress.com/promo/tendollars to purchase your companion eBook.

Apress®
THE EXPERT'S VOICE™